BELMONT

Books by Stephen Burt

POETRY

Belmont
Parallel Play
Popular Music

NONFICTION

The Art of the Sonnet
Close Calls with Nonsense: Reading New Poetry
The Forms of Youth: Twentieth-Century Poetry and Adolescence
Randall Jarrell and His Age

BELMONT

Poems

STEPHEN BURT

Graywolf Press

This publication is made possible, in part, by the voters of Minnesota through a Minnesota State Arts Board Operating Support grant, thanks to a legislative appropriation from the arts and cultural heritage fund, and through a grant from the National Endowment for the Arts. Significant support has also been provided by Target, the McKnight Foundation, Amazon.com, and other generous contributions from foundations, corporations, and individuals. To these organizations and individuals we offer our heartfelt thanks.

Published by Graywolf Press
250 Third Avenue North, Suite 600
Minneapolis, Minnesota 55401

www.graywolfpress.org

Published in the United States of America

ISBN 978-1-55597-644-6

2 4 6 8 9 7 5 3 1
First Graywolf Printing, 2013

Library of Congress Control Number: 2013931483

Cover design: Kapo Ng @ A-Men Project

Cover photo: Kromkrathog, Shutterstock

ACKNOWLEDGMENTS

My thanks to the journals, magazines, websites, anthologies, and chap-book publishers that have printed, reprinted or adapted many of these poems, sometimes in earlier versions:

AGNI, Almost Island, At Length, The Awl, Barrow Street, Battersea Review, Boston Review, Catch-Up, Colorado Review, Congeries, Diagram, Drunken Boat, Elixir, Fulcrum, Gallous, Gulf Coast, Harvard Review, Hilobrow, InDigest, International Literary Quarterly (ILQ), The Journal (Ohio), Like Starlings, The Literary Review (NJ), London Review of Books, New Haven Review, New Ohio Review, The New Yorker, Oxford Poetry, Pleiades, Ploughshares, PN Review, Poetry Daily (poems.com), 32 Poems, The Poker, Slate, Southwest Review, Verse Daily (versedaily.com), The Yale Review.

Motionpoems; The Pushcart Prize: Best of the Small Presses; Connecting Lines: New Poetry from Mexico, ed. Forrest Gander; *Diagram 4,* ed. Ander Monson; *Homewrecker!,* ed. Daphne Gottlieb; *Old Flame: From the First Ten Years of 32 Poems,* ed. John Poch, Deborah Ager, and Bill Beverly; *Tower Poetry Miscellany,* ed. Peter McDonald; *Troubling the Line: Trans and Genderqueer Poetry and Poetics,* ed. TC Tolbert and Tim Trace Peterson; *The Unexpected Guest,* ed. Sally Tallant and Paul Domella.

Shot Clocks: Poems for the WNBA (New York: Harry Tankoos, 2006).

*for Jessie
and Nathan
and Cooper
together*

CONTENTS

3

Come, you and I will thither presently;
And in the morning early we will both
Fly toward Belmont.

—*The Merchant of Venice*

POEM OF NINE A.M.

Sing for us whose troubles

are troubles we're lucky to have:
cold orange juice, and cold coffee,

corridor after corridor, as our
circadian rhythms fall into place:

work is a refuge from home, and home from work.
We have task force reports,

but no tasks, and no force,
so far removed from concrete and crisp air

we might be living anywhere,
enjoying each other's company, within bounds.

• • •

When I flew over the Grand Canyon, I loved—
who wouldn't?—to see the majestic gash in earth,

but what *moved* me
were the flat hints of grids

that began and ended several miles away,
tan, ecru, beige, knife-scratches on dry toast,

and then houses—some might have been trailers—so faint

and isolated next to those faint lines.
Single grains of sugar. Sesame seeds.

We should never look down
on what gives strangers comfort,

on what we learn too late that we might need.

1

It's not, as scientists used to think, that children can't tell the difference between the real world and the imaginary world. . . . It's just that they don't see any particular reason for preferring to live in the real one.

—Alison Gopnik, *The Philosophical Baby*

THE PEOPLE ON THE BUS

We have had our lives.
The reservoir visible
In the window beside our elbows, and the willow
Branches trailing at our stop
Are the nature we leave
Behind us gladly, since it has no place

For all we have recently learned: that sex
Is temporary, help
Ours to hand down now, and materials science
Not the only kind. We thank
Calm, careful Minerva, goddess
Of adults, who for so many years took us

To school: her voice the timbre of fretless bass,
Her eyes the color of pencil lead, she taught
Us how to behave in order to have our rewards
In twenty years. We have them, and if we wish
Too often, this fall, to have led another life
We do not mean that we would give up ours:

Though we stand in a row and sway
Before an obstructed view, we are able to find
Initials outlined in the crosshatched trees,
And pebbles—calculi—around our ponds
And cherish them; we like to watch the roads
Along which the perennial pollen sifts down

As finely as ever, making a soft powder
Of brass amid the troughs in softball fields.
Our skills are finally in demand.
If you mock us, Pan,
In whom we also believe, do it
As gently as you can.

NATHAN

No baby yet; instead, our gentle house
accumulates blankets, slipsheets, pillows, strings
and ripening traces of seemingly infinite snow
confirming itself to itself in near-silence, its work
to take the edge off nearly everything.
Jessie can still drive, can't drive, can drive,
enjoys and despises these weeks between baby and job.
The sky at noon stunned us, paler than any page.
We got in the car as if off to search for the sun.

• • •

Unaccustomed sunlight tops the State Capitol's

snowy dome as seen from the birthing room. Our water broke at ten.

We take contractions as they come, or don't come.

In Russia, birches bend with hostile winds.

"There's never a place to put stuff in these rooms,

"with people always running in and running out."

Come home, come into this, thy world.

• • •

As when, night-driving through the jagged up-
land shelves of Pennsylvania,
the axe-blade tops of hills a threat or shade
within a shade, moonlit uncertainties
and too-fast trucks descending one lane off

as you ascend, determined but in fear,
the last high switchbacks to the looming ridge,
the road reverses, and the eastern view
exposes an orange sky, and all the hills
are gentle slope and natural descent,
and clearly marked, and even newly paved,
and even the steering wheel's last notch and scratch
and beveled case seems part of the design—
no glare, no blur, no chill, no shade, the green
treetops preserved: safe the road through and down,
the sun's announcement of their separateness
the first safe moment of your whole trip home—
so, Nathan, was your birth today at dawn.

• • •

The sun   some coin   in an unfocused eye
the juvenile ghost   of winter lifts
our striving houses   frost in soil   hard trying
to move earth by installments   and so soon

Oh oracle   where to land now   what map
what glare what windows   driveways   attic rooms
what mansards   what Cape Cods   what arts and crafts
what will you build   what if you too grow up

• • •

The size of a loaf of bread and about as warm,
you take a serious interest in the breast,
not as a kind of nutrition, but as the world's
preeminent source of softness and of rest.
Toes peeling, fingers seeking happiness,

you look up to us and upon us as if only we
could tell you where you came from, what to be,
and whether the swaddled boy and cloth-bound girl
now visible from your window will do you harm.

． ． ．

Not John Keats' "Ode on Indolence"
but Ezra Jack Keats' immortal *The Snowy Day*.
Not the snowy litter that blocks our walks
but the snow-laden wind that scatters our unopened bills
and cards among the other scraps at play.

Not the evolutionary sense
of hiccups, as a relict or reflex
from the years when all of us had gills,
but the overwhelming evidence
that our very small child intends
far more than we can think, or see, or say.

BELMONT OVERTURE (POEM OF EIGHT A.M.)

It's about settling down and settling in
      and trying not to settle for,

about three miles from the urban core,
      where the not-quite-wild bald turkey, looking so lost

and inquisitive next to the stop for the 74,
      peers into the roseless rosebush, up at the pointless oar

above one townhouse's swept steps, and the US
      and floral and nautical flags flaunt their calm semaphore.

Walking past them, today, with our stroller, we note as we pass
      the wreath of real twigs on our next-door neighbor's door

and beside it another, not sold in any store,
      made of pipecleaners and plastic oak leaves. It looks like a nest,

something Nathan could put together, with the rest
      of his gregarious preschool class . . .

We have learned to carry, everywhere, sunscreen,
      and insect repellent, and pretzel sticks, and Aquafor

in case any shrubs scratch the kids. We mean
      it when we say we like it; we feel sure

it's safe around here, and once we feel safe, it's our nature
      to say we're unsatisfied, and pretend to seek more.

TO SUBARUS

In poems autobiographical information serves the same purpose as references to birch trees or happiness or Subarus.

—David Orr, *The New York Times Book Review,* July 20, 2008

Whose silver is lead in sunlight, whose maroon
looks like the rust on a storm drain,
whose popular Forester also comes
in dead pine-needle green,
with rounded roof and trapezoidal frame,
you seem to mean

that I will never surprise anybody again.
So studiously unglamorous, at rest
in our one-car driveway, you seem to claim
that to be adult is simply to care less
about doing your own thing on your own,
and more about what other people require:
to care less for the space cleared by new brooms,

for the fast lane and the fine line
that might, or might not, separate
romance from folly, and more
for Dr. Harvey Karp, who taught new parents how to calm
their infants with attempts to recreate
the volume and vibrations of the womb.

REVERSE DECIDUOUS EXISTENCE

We meerkats are all smiles
As we stand again on thin feet
Taking a break from the sand
Through which we are delighted to scroll for grubs
And roll at night into warmer burrows. Scratch that:
Our pictures of ourselves as animals
Gives pleasure or cuteness
But neither responsibility nor joy
And joy is what I want to confer
Today, small joy in some
Windy quality of a household,
The household of Nathan's boots, for example, which he
Takes off with help, names with verve, and loves to invert
Although they too are full of sand.
We give him a hand.
You see what just happened? I can't
Put an anecdote down without folding the temperate
Seasons, like compliant sofabeds,
All up in our subjective day: O season of nutmeg,
Season of multiple naptimes, season
Of 9:09 (a.m. and p.m.), single
Season in which happiness writes
Off-white, and paints
With great Robert Ryman swaths,
Chalk, chromium, yogurt, silicon dioxide, sand again.
It must be harder
To be a baby than to be ourselves
And harder still to live in the unfolded desert,
Tracked by scientists, groutless, to live as prey,
Just temporarily bipedal,
In warrens which do not drive our cousins away.

As for us, we live in our reverse
Deciduous existences,
Covered in solid colors every
Winter, which we shed in stacks each year.

PEONIES

       Yes, another
poem about flowers and kids. Our son
       thinks this one is a ball,
or full of balls: like jesters' caps with bells,
one for each stem, or old pawnbrokers' signs,
the lot next door in rainy April weather
dangles, and then in sunlight lifts, what he
believes he ought to pluck and grasp and throw,

if we would let him. Little does he know
       how each bud, given cues
from symbiotic ants, will open up
pink surface after surface, flagrant scraps
of incandescent fabric coming loose
like grownups' lives or last month's local news,
like promises, or generosity,
or overuse. So soon it isn't fair,

what he could take in his small fist all spring
and shake in anger when we told him no—
that is, *don't touch them*—nods, and will agree
to share its colors; still unraveling,
       curled up against its core,
each of the heavy flowers starts to be
a casualty of gravity, so low
it looks ashamed, as if the earth expected more.

EXPLORING THE SUBURBS

It makes a certain sort of sense—
you don't have to like every flower you see, for example,
but you do have to give it a try;
clover blooms with their blanched
and tiniest petals, like architectural models
or a child's diagram
in a world built only for children, who keep going wrong,
yanking the wrists of distracted caretakers, not knowing
the only real world is the one they have. It is shaped
more or less like an olive, round
but irregular nevertheless, and tangy inside.
They put in something extra for the parents,
vague, but worth advertising: its nickname is *silence*,
its value tallied only after the fact.

Inside, as in a snow globe,
we saw a cheerful row of wooden
pallets holding up stacked 2x4s,
good omens for an otherwise difficult day,
portending tax overrides, storms over school construction,
a fortune in confusion, wisdom's end.
Why, for example, *do sports people
have numbers on their backs?*
*Where do the buses go
when they go home?* The agile flag
in our park is happy to pick up the toddlers' questions
and store them in its ever-popular roots.

But they *are* us,
that's what they say.

POEM OF SEVEN A.M.

The tireless & endless rubbish on & against the curb
looks to have been the product of a bilious regime
unknown to human motives, & too big for human hands:
these cylinders like fuselages, paper-bag tombstones
with trails like moths, like flak, began their arduous crawls
to death & transfiguration the day before yesterday,
awaiting the local recycling, which has not yet come.
They dwarf us, although we have carried them out; they build,
indifferently, our tombs, & yet as we work behind
them we can take pride in their confounding extent,
since they claim that we pick up after ourselves. The stacks
of cardboard we folded up, then split with Exacto knives
into a kind of dismembered Northern Renaissance altarpiece;
horseradish; a hash of shredded paper; shredded dregs
of cooking lessons; crushed acrylic cylinders and tubes;
a box that a kitten could sleep in; three gunmetal wheels
that roll nowhere: all come together in hasty concert
to make of their parts a demented harmonium, where
the wind is no longer opposed to our presence, but sings
loud etudes as we pump the footpedals and watch
our block become an auditorium, whose broad
countermelodies carry low tones the pigeons may hear
above their gutters' chatter, & then again attend
to such repeated anthems for our neighborhood, our home.

TO AUTUMN

Trash instead of geese
Has landed all over our pond!
Single sheets of newsprint lie apart
Or overlap, as if collecting dew:
Our son, who has come here
In a stroller to applaud birds,

Applauds their absence, stands, and picks up rocks,
Enumerating: *One, two, three,*
Four, seven, eight.
               This year our summer lasts
Until October, an unhealthy state
Of which we take advantage, taking walks
That last all morning, making pebbled tracks,
Staying away from the road. Meanwhile big trucks

Patrol our Concord Avenue, their red
Sides' single question flourishing
In circus script, like handbills' old good news:
"Who But W. B. Mason?"
Who indeed.
               Yellow clover abides
Beside all our footpaths. Hundreds of miles away
Last night, a tumultuous infestation of gnats

Shut down, for over an hour, a baseball game.
The Indians won. An opaque, sticky cloud
Befuddled the pitchers no end.
By then we were almost asleep,
Myself, and Jessie, and Nathan in his crib,
Guarded by his fortification of blankets,
For whose instruction our slow world was made.

COLOR THEORY

How yellow the sky how little the understanding

Intangible the things we know for sure

Dusty silica clouds over Europe the very same day

We brought our Cooper home   His second   Too yellow

For comfort   Too sleepy   Just sleepy enough

For us to sleep ourselves   That was last night

Today the clouds shift   Outside shifts   Rain and shadows

A mezzotint glow   Then no glow   Heart or soul

Exactly seven pounds of civilization

Hematochrome and skin and bilirubin

Yawns   blinks and can't make up   his made-up mind

The atmosphere can't keep its own eyes open

We can't keep our own eyes closed

WORDS FOR TEA TOWELS

People have good reasons
For the things they do.
No one spends a morning
Thinking just of you.

Nothing's worth a quarrel,
So the fractious say.
If they can persuade you
They can have their way.

Children learn by slogans.
Grownups (that is, us)
Learn to cease to question,
Take without a fuss.

Nothing's worth the bother.
Never start a fight;
If you feel neglected
You've done something right.

Fun is for the very
Fortunate, and few.
People have good reasons
For the things they do.

THE TASK

The person you expect to be next year
Is less heroic than you are, more glum,
With fewer talismans. He praises the day even so.
If this world has fallen together by chance
And evolution, she says, *it is*
A marvel, but if somebody
Designed it, yikes!
Dear shepherd: do you have a staff?
Dear effortful ones: how far are you wandering home?
Do you prefer paper or plastic homes
For purchase? Can you fit on the head of a match?

These days, though, every corridor is a flooded
Mangrove swamp, where ancient types despise
Our white-collar competition, our scandalous talk.
There's a filter on our enjoyment: it kicks in
Between twilight and dearly-
Beloved, if less respectable,
Dawn. The sun shows that
We already owe too much. And still hope prepares
Itself like a breadknife left in bread, like wooden
Models in the kitchen trap,
For the caustic gift of trying
To imagine how it would feel, or what you would
Do, if one day you were really
In charge. The enemies
Of the naiads remain on guard
Over 24 hours per day, archaic rules
And halberds at the ready: you must
Listen to them. You must not do as they say.

SUNDAY AFTERNOON

When all the kids babies and grownups are napping at naptime
      and sleep well during the day
it is a masterpiece, there are trombones
      and harps in order, banjos, hosannas in Heaven
and orchestras tune up and start to play
      an instrumental hymn of jubilee,
very quietly, so as not to wake the babies.

"WHEN THE SWEET WIND DID GENTLY KISS THE TREES"

So tired of shining, glowing, sparkling things,
   leaves, grass and moons in moonlight—so many queries,
so much starlit punctuation, so many
   tiny theodicies, wishful thoughts,
like sprinkles on a spoiled cake.

The night is burnt orange. It was never ours.
   Nobody sensible wants to run away.

You don't just decide
   to become a different person,
but realize that you have become the person you are—
   not who you were, not who you want to be,
but something close to them, in exactly the way
   the new low-intensity streetlights come close to the moon.

FIRST ASTRONOMY GLOBE

Incapable of glowing
under my own light, I spin
instead. I do my best work when you are in bed,
either quiet & wide-eyed, or else asleep & unknowing,
& though I have an infinite supply
of darkness & silence, I let it all go by,
preferring not to scare you with the void.
I cut up my space into parts, & the parts fit in
to stories: *the boy who grew a giant fin,*
for example, & others you made up, *the anteater's tail,*
the trapezoid you named *the cellular phone*—
absurd or anachronistic, but no more so
than the camel, the hunter's belt and torso,
the dog star, the giant ladle, the lesser whale,
a cross to light the flags of southerly nations.
A wise
young gazer will memorize
not just the names for made-up constellations—
those dotted lines, those rules religions trace—
but the ranks of the stars themselves: keeping close to my face,
the attentive child past his bedtime sees
dim numbers that connect the faintest dots
to their glow-in-the-dark parameters, the plots
that cut my sphere
into right angles, minutes and degrees.
He finds in that firmament
no sign of human intent,
not even to ask what we are doing here.

OWL MUSIC

Who who
        were you yesterday
in the starless night   *   where did you go
        Who who do you hear   *   can you come with me

The crickety summer deceives us   *   underneath
        so many   *   a swath of pollen and haze
So many individuals so many
        stridulations   *   so many retrograde eyes

At sundown it seems harder   *   to eat the air
        than live the same way every day
so we take flight   *   owl music
        pinions and talons   *   into the harmless night
Who who stays hungry   *   who will scare

Who will resent my camouflage
        my plumage   *   my desire for concealment
my predatory and nearly inaudible work
        not wise but able to look down
over mammals   *   their scurry their scary delay

Only to strangers   *   to those who will never see you
        can you say what you believe
Who who
        will hear an owl credo:

I have run from and risen from the real and dimly
        adumbrated shapes of suburban things
and then run back to them   I believe with ease

in things that nobody can see
but not in what I cannot hear

I do not believe that art is a form of religion
            an unforgivable selfishness that takes
the time I always owe to other people
            I do not quite believe it but I have come close

I have seen my own span of attention
            shrunk to a burnt lightbulb's tungsten wire
lit like a pinpoint star on the back of a spoon
            a spiderweb concatenation
a matrix of expiation
            a mock-up of a better nation   *   a trap to catch flies
and songs come at naptime or else   *   at the end of a day
            miniscule in endless promises
to find a way out of the Klein bottle   *   out of the air
            nachtmusik   *   dignified spotlight

Who who threw
            these deteriorating clothes
into their heap mound on mound
            by the noble creekbed
amid the curious insects wet logs sticks
where pine needles scatter   *   their scent rises over the common
tracing and tracing across the private lawn

The crickets claim subscriber rights
            their comforting abrasive ring
black handle up and down   *   on a rotary phone
            we could not bring ourselves to throw away
It too lies

where horse chestnuts prickle the dark
shells split like pillowcases   *   nothing inside

Who who
          would keep eyes closed
Who would not want
          to suck on a thumb   *   to become
an animal that you could sing to sleep
          although the mind fades   *   its recollections fade
sex and death whatever they were   *   fade
          as the morning stars regard the moon

and the automobiles out of sight along Route Two

stay asleep in their noise   *   owl music continues
          underneath the overhead
and baffles itself in descent   *   to scan the ground

Who who comes down to see
          who gets to know
all this raw dirt   *   all this assertive script
          of tangled rootlets   small asseverations
one oak's new fibers reach down just to make
          some shelter for another   seedling seedling
seedling seedling seedling seed

Your cover is shallow   you grown-up
          you like it that way
You get ten minutes to yourself   at dawn
          before the creek wakes up again

POEM OF SIX A.M.

One child wakes up when the other has gone

back to bed, if not to sleep. One more false dawn
slaps you, pink bedroom window, but I have no right to complain:
you have no choice but to begin the day for me.

. . .

Lead on, lead on,
fortissimo washer and dryer, mechanical train
in our unfinished basement: who else could play for me

your wild snare, your floor tom and your gong,
their rough polyrhythms, subordinate quarter and main
beat? Who keeps the darks from turning gray for me?

. . .

With pick and carabiners and crampon
the climbers ascend the assiduous counterpane,
whose rising sun lets out a single ray for me.

. . .

There is also a song
made of Cheerios, honey nut and multigrain,
oats, rice, wheat, corn and barley. Nobody should pay for me;

we can afford it. Soon I will enter a zone
of bananas and yogurt and plastic forks, propane
tanks, and cheese wheels, wrapped and set out on a tray for me.

. . .

Who learned to be strong
without self-pity? How did they learn to contain
the impulse to fight or to flee? Who else will lay for me

the useless ghosts of independent men,
the superheroic, the Villon, the Dylan, the villain,
such lumber, such figures, so many to clear away for me?

A SOCK IS NOT A HUMAN BEING

because it is a sock, begins
the poem Nathan asked me to write, dictating
the title and first line, or half the first line (see above):
a sock is not a human being, being
unable to cry, burn dinner, forget to buy
dinner, or spread marmalade on toast.
It can't select clothes or get dressed in them or bathe itself,
nor does it interrupt me with shocking comments
in order to get the rest of us to take note.

Although a sock can flaunt a personal style,
a sock is not a human being: no sock,
tube or dress-up, thick, fitted or frilly, argyle
or peppermint-striped, has ever gone home at noon
on its own, nor been sent home in order to change.
No sock can choose to run or not to run
or not to have a run, or wait to run,
for example, behind the final stand of pines
by the tremulous reservoir, brushing itself off the sand.

A sock can wear out, or wear art.
A sock can be torn apart
by the passage of time or sharp objects; it may not object
to harsh words, if that's how it's always been addressed.
A sock will never ask you for a rest.

Some socks are masks,
with spangles woven on, or felt-tip pen.
If they have real names, no one ever asks.
They say what we make them say, whether they understand
much or any of it. In this way they resemble our friends.

There are socks in this world that have tried too hard to fit in.
No sock, however, believes in original sin;
only some see a terrible split between women and men,
boys and girls, kinds of grown-ups, principally expressed
by decisions about which basket, drawer or bin.

You can speak through your hat and pretend not to mean what you say,
or speak like a sock with great flat button eyes, matte-
black, tortoiseshell, magenta, or medium gray.
Not I, not I, says the sock, but the hand
that speaks through me, however reluctantly,
becomes the judge and wins the day.

2

It was as if she had an appointment to meet the rest of herself, sometime, somewhere. . . . Perhaps each of them concealed another person in himself, just as she did.

—Willa Cather, *The Song of the Lark*

THE PARAPHILIA ODES

1

O my companions in microfiber & leather
O my companions in spangle & tulle
O my companions   cat carriers in hand
Great treasure has been given to you to lose

2

Nothing holy is real.
Renunciation is the new appeal.

Our memories don ratty water wings
And slap and flail their way across our pond.

At thirteen we learned to hide in their closets and listen
As if we could learn from the latest, the most secret noise.

Who did we love? Not the ones who returned our first calls:
By the end of each year we had to prove ourselves

Again. We never did. This poem, like all poems,
Takes place entirely in school. It has

Left the sensuous details entirely for the next section
Which cannot assemble them, not even with you.

3

He follows the tiny bones
      At the beloved's wrist,
           Their workings as she writes on posterboard.

Candycane polish flakes from one toenail.
    The alluvial fan of the bones at the top of the foot
        Slides inwards as his bare toe touches hers.

She has cut off the collar from her Izod shirt
    So that it exposes her clavicle, then falls straight
        Along her ribs. He feels them when they kiss.

It is the deviations from the script
    Of her body and his, the absences and
        Mistakes, that excite him most:

The sweat that darkens the crotch
    Of her flat, plaid, red-on-green
        Underpants whose cotton has worn smooth,

The slack elastic at the waist, through which,
    All too gingerly, she leads his palm.
        The two of them stop

There. He will always stop there.
    He will ask his future lovers for nothing else,
        And nothing more, and nothing less.

4

The Fall is not the discovery of sin but the discovery of responsibilities, consequential, open-ended or indefinite: the mere knowledge of good and evil is itself the end of a kind of joy, since we are so made as to let that knowledge guide us, or at least to pretend that it does, to strive for at least the appearance of favoring others' pleasure over our own. (Eve did not give up anything for Adam before the discovery of the apple, nor did he ever ask that she do so.) As we grow we fall deeper, accumulating, and recalling, ever more obligations; we therefore see people younger than we are (rightly or wrongly) as lacking them, and long for the faraway time in our own lives when we believe we could have acted selfishly without knowing that acting selfishly was wrong. We therefore encourage our friends and partners, as adults, to become or remain more childlike than we believe ourselves to be, not only because we can guide them (hence participate vicariously in their pleasures) but because we feel guilty about our own desires as we do not feel guilty about theirs—in the imagined economy of eros, ambition, assistance and self-denial, *their* desires do not necessarily interfere with *our* obligations. And so we take greater pleasure, for much of our lives, in helping our friends or partners get what they want than we do in taking what we want for ourselves.

5

Barely aware how I melt   *   in this warm

Light   *   let me lie with   *   my wet secret don't make me

Tell   *   skin feels slippery   *   so I can't

Speak   *   only cry   *   the plastic mattress cover held

Me up   *   from the balls of my feet   *   rough crinkly

Clings around my hips   *   my diaper my   *   rubber pants
    keeping me safe

In my night sleepy   *   swaddling where I am

Held   *   have I wet   *   the bed   *   am I

Asleep   *   if I wake   *   the caudal bone

Still wet   *   where I wet   *   myself   *   between my

Legs   *   some part is lost   *   the rest   *   wash me

Away let me fall   *   on bare knees   *   out of bed dress me

Up   *   undress me make   *   me sleepy again make   *
   me into your tiny

Possession   *   make me   *   someone new

6

Fake fish outside the sex-toy store (inside
Its story-high front window) swim around
On strings, on strings; their pulleys rise indoors
To circle in midair, on a blue scrim
Lit up to look like water—corals, moss,
A diver's rusty effigy. Inside,
Fluorescence says, we shop below the waves—
The fuchsia, pea-green, ultramarine

Subsurfaces and trenches of desire . . .
What could these scarlet thigh-highs do, equipped
As each one is, with batteries and lights?
Who would these leather socks and kerchiefs please?
The laws of natural history are exact
As laws of pleasure: just this, nothing else,
No other fabric, chain or term of art
Controls the night or makes observers grin.

From their evolved mosaic underground
At 81st Street Station, trilobite

And Gila monster, shark and bowerbird
Stare out to where cold passengers meet trains:
Weighed down with bright-eyed shopping, our sex toys
Still heavy in our bags, we disembark
To meet the eyes of creatures who meets ours
As if to ask us: *How do you get off?*

STEPHANIE

An orange nylon collar, a scallop-shell A-cup, worn tortoiseshell
buttons that pop off a dress,
   my own . . .

This world is too good for us, and would be intolerable
if we could not imagine another just like it

in which we could get, and reject, another chance.

IODINE

As children we yearned for companionship of some sort but never knew what sort; as teens, we knew but found it uncomfortably elusive, tangled behind bed-curtains for inappropriate rooms, at parties under catty-corner basement stairs, behind doors hung off true, or in the rose light of school darkrooms where no one develops unless they first copy the key. The colorless ideas of more recent years still sleep furiously inside us, submerged in their fixer, close at hand. Some problems don't have solutions. And yet we live now, and try to tell one another that we live as we want to live now, surrounded not by the people we hoped to meet some years ago, but by their well-meant and importunate demands. Go away! Find us space! we almost say, but never intend to say, as if all our wishes could realize themselves should we only take back our grotty crawlspaces without sacrificing what we earned since then, as if we had wrapped ourselves in our own old news, preserving desires until the year or the hour when we could open them up and begin to learn what they are.

RUE

sometimes, however, to be a "ruined man" is itself a vocation.
                    —T. S. Eliot

When he refastened the opalescent plastic
                    buttons on her button-down shirt,
he misaligned most of them. She had to do it again.
What if somebody else
                    near the back of the bus had seen?

I overheard Melissa say, "I'm tired
                    of everyone calling me Goody."
I didn't know.
                    Later that year,
the Ramones began recording *Road to Ruin*.
It had a new drummer, a lot more backup vocals,
the same no-nonsense pace, the all-male sound.

Gossip in school makes a kind of electrical storm,
or else
        a medium of exchange:
once you share what you know, then you learn what you can.

The Ramones were not boys.
                    The ruin of *boy* is *man*.

In junior high we drew
                    on almost everything,
incising, chiding, wielding ballpoint pens—
the scratchy reptile-hide seats
                    with torn-out safety belts,
the denim that made ladders up our jeans . . .
small flowers, boxy video game

42

protagonists, raindrops, capital letters, things
that girls thought scandalous,
                    boys thought obscene.

What else I heard I would not say,
wishing I were a girl,
                    or had ever been a girl,
or like a girl had secrets for some body to betray.

Road to Ruin had the Ramones' first
cover, the Searchers' yearning "Needles and Pins,"
in which the boy says he "saw the face of love, and I knew
                    I had to run away."

We were there, in the bus. I wanted to stay.

FICTITIOUS GIRL RAISED BY CATS

They loved to ignore me. I loved to be ignored.
Because my mother and father asked too much
on my behalf, because their fine ideas
of my incipient perfection tasted

sour on my tongue like endless need,
because their silvered glass and dinnerware
shone far too brightly on us, and because
my sisters were never permitted to lick them clean,

I ran behind the house to live with strays.
Curled up in jungle gyms, storm drains, cool eaves,
we slept through winter sunshine, out of sight.
In grilling season, we dragged ruby meats,

our salvaged treasure, out the shady doors
of unlocked ramblers, and fought over them.
I learned to leap decisively from curbs,
to clamber to the end of every branch,

never to wait for rescue. We had left
our skittish footprints in the mounds of sand
the lips of driveways gathered every spring,
but nothing else to prove we were alive.

I kept my bright pink overalls, old words
for *eat* and *sleep* and *shelter* and *come down*,
and an affection that was the price of nothing,
given and taken freely, as if on a whim.

FOR AVRIL LAVIGNE

I used to be told
just what to play, and how to play:
I was wide-eyed
for the halides, the emerald tides
of applause, raccoon-eyed in the foreign sun.
That's the thing about spotlights: it hurts when they leave you alone.

Now I feel old:
at least nineteen, today.
It gets hard to decide
who to be: minx, brides-
maid, pirate, tagger, ghost, in search of more fun
than I could be when I was my first name, blank as cut stone.

Dad, I want to say thanks
for forcing me to practice
every night after school. It's hard to postpone
what you want for what you will want later, to put things off
when you might change so much from each March to that May,
but now I know you have to study so hard to sound free,

and if everyone thinks
I'm fake, Goth-lite, black lace
and tennis shoes and butterflies drawn
on denim in ballpoint, it is almost enough
to know all of you pay me attention: I will say
that I'm crazy, I'm yours, I'm real, I'm lost, but the me

that I want to keep is the one that dictated the mix,
the author of gold-notebook storyboards, not the star turn:
the planner in the mirror, the overhearer
who once stood in line for so long, who wanted to learn
the secrets, the customs, the costumes, the whole bag of tricks.

DRAFT CAMP

for the WNBA

We are specialists of sorts, or out of sorts. Too many people care what we are wearing.

One of us could spot a wren on a dare in a darkening glade from sixty yards away. One of us can lift any four others. One of us died. One of us stops conversations with her hawkish malachite-green eyes.

We have had repeatedly to admit that we are individual bodies, roaming through contested, crowded space, and then to believe we are part of one another, enrolled in very temporary combinations, minute-to-minute teams.

And why shouldn't everyone hope to be selected? Don't we all wait through life, *choose me, choose me?*

One of us can snap almost any tree limb. Another can be a tree, hard to get over, almost impossible to see around. Most of us have been called and called again.

One of us can draw blood with a glance. One can steal the sides off a scalene triangle, the green off any leaf, pickpocket the oxygen out of the air. Some of us have worked and traveled past the point of diminishing returns.

One and only one will be remembered in 25 years, her number hoisted up like constellations, winched and fixed in an indoor sky.

And why shouldn't everyone hope to be selected? Don't we all wait through life, *choose me, choose me?*

TWO VICTORIAN SCENES

Lady Clementina Hawarden (1822–65)

1

They stand or lie
Beside themselves, in frame
After frame, constrained
By the requirements of an inexpert
Elegance they do not wish to look
As if they had mastered so soon. Before
Their inviting bay window in Kensington, loud stripes
And sun fall hard on one
Another, perhaps fifteen
Degrees from true, as the heat of the patient day
Spreads over the younger sister, Clementine,
Whose sleepy form—almost
An odalisque—soaks up the foreground while Isabel
Leans forward, keeping
Watch, herself still watched
By lilacs, a mirror, particulate
Summer air. Nothing you know
Will last much longer, not even the tiny stars
In the fabric of the sky, much less this sky-
Like drapery, which has no end
In view. Out of sight among
Black curtains, a mother and
Photographer tries to focus just
On what she sees, and never to see too far.

2

They sip sharp tea: we see the whole
Salon, whose rueful maroons
Encourage our calm, as if destiny were a set

Dresser, its chalice left up
On a broad credenza, giving the girls
One present between them, meaning, for daughters, *grow up*
Or else, for mothers (and for fathers, though none
Appear), *learn as soon as you can*
Bring yourself to learn how soon they will
Not need you. Added long
After development, brushed-in
Tints neither falsify the high, thick
Taffeta of their gowns, nor much impinge
On their receding curves; a statuette
Of Victory rises behind the egg-and-dart
Mantel as a yolk-yellow
Tempera moon in crescent bruises her heel.
Lady Hawarden posed her two daughters in frame after frame
Deliberately, from the angle of their
Ankles to the turn of their fine chins,
So that they seem to belong to each other, and look
Only inwards, away
From colors as such, into the undefined
Air or vanishing point, as if to say:
Our mother knew
Us as well as anyone
Has, but what did she know?
And Lady Hawarden held
Them up as if to respond:
Tonight you may venture out
Of doors, but now there is light
We must not waste. Please stay just as you are.

LITTLE LAMENT FOR THE LEGION OF SUPER-HEROES

Too many to list, but we recognized them all
Among each issue's battles: Saturn Girl
Wore white and red; read minds; once quit the team
And let her teenage colleagues try to save
The 30th century from shape-shifters, ghosts,
Illusionists whose eyes ate through the page.

Without his armor on, sad Wildfire
Was nothing but a bright electric blur;
His flashy powers weighed less on his mind
Than flesh or blood he lacked. Shrinking Violet
Hid safe below a fight, then, from beneath
A villain's notice, would grow up so fast
One punch as she arose laid bad guys low.

On covers, in collectors' see-through bags,
In close-formation flight (like kites, like geese)
Arrayed for fans to find and name each one,
We knew you by your logos, stripes and capes;
You knew how long we wished we could dispel
What we were called at home—the middle-school
Kingdom of terms clapped on us like applause,
Which, fastening on us, tell us we serve,
And let our powers go . . .
                                    The future's kids
Could name themselves: a wish under whose laws
The powers to burn metals like small suns
And to make one's own body helium
Are the same gift—the talent equally
Of winged Dawnstar; magnetic Cosmic Boy
And Matter-Eater Lad; Braniac Five;
Chameleon Boy. Light Lass. Star Boy. Dream Girl.

BAD NEWZ

Alec Soth: "Kenny and Bill—Bad Newz, Grand Rapids, Minnesota"

They tilt their guitars and stare.
Each boy puts one foot toward
Us, one where a trailing wire
Would run to an amplifier
If amplifiers were there.
Bill's Gibson glitters like ore.
Kenny's Ibañez hoards

White noise in its black fretboard.
Bill's double chin shows. Is it fair
To mention his pudge? Kenny's hair
Gets stuck behind one ear.
Each of the brothers wears
A T-shirt, loose jeans, and a pair
Of bruised high-tops. A pear-

Shaped garbage bag hugs a steel bar.
The big rectangular blur
Behind them looks like the door
To a walk-in refrigerator.
Maybe dad is a restaurateur,
A diner owner who requires
Kenny to spend six hours

A week moving cases of beer,
While Bill chops potatoes, or scours
Grease from the checkerboard floor.
Bill imagines a national tour:
CBGB's. The Black Cat. Hardcore.
Or metal: the glow and allure
Of arenas and open-air

Pyrotechnics at dusk, a chauffeur.
Or do they hope modestly for
Sideman jobs, L.A. 'burbs, the secure
Work of studio engineers?
Two boys hold two guitars
In a basement kitchen, and care
What you think of them. Next year

They promise to practice more.
Right now their repertoire
Is six songs, seven chords,
Five originals, and a spare
Reworking of REM's four-
Minute anthem about a lost car:
"Can't Get There from Here."

SO LET AM NOT

Subjunctive lost bangles and butterfly clips, plastic
        sapphires, sparkle barrettes that I used to wear
in my all too short hair
        not withstanding, I am not a flirty girl.
Weeds like washcloths and silky flags bloom on the front and back lawns
        as if recreating a sort of green room
outdoors, as if the natural spot-
        light would let
me take part in its show,
        let my crinoline or perhaps
my taffeta go,
        although
I have never been that flirty girl.

I would have had colorless eyes,
        approximating a ghost,
though sadly eager to please, like a seal.
        I get dismissed,
dismantled or dismayed
        in the late low-intensity light by the summertime real.

Now I get out of bed
        at sunrise, and am part
of others, of responsibilities.
        I do not want
to pull up roots or build a new
        high house amid imaginary trees.

But sometimes in lengthening sunlight
        my silhouette on the pavement
has not a care in the world
        except for volleyball (set, spike, point, gain)
and popularity . . .

I would flaunt a bottleglass-green
artificiality,
  one streak in my straight-line hair.
I could learn makeup
  badly, with a geek-girl flair
for I'll-be-there and I-don't-care,
  and when I get off the 86 bus I can see by the parking lot's
storm drain, before my feet,
  a coin: one side is rusty, incomplete,
a profile of some guy who united his states,
  and to that history I say "sweet,
but I can see myself nowhere."
  And yet it is a feeling I prefer
to the other side, the faceless and the
  valueless, the absolutely free.

My blood runs fuchsia,
  no, chartreuse.
I still prefer,
  rather than feeling
beautiful, to be of use.

  So let yourself be
but know who you seem.
  Know the difference
between a dream and a dream.
  This poem makes eyes at you,
eyes back at me.
  It cannot be
whatever it wants to be,
  though it can flirt.
It is flat and is made of ink and it cannot hurt.

I could go on.
The moon could mean dawn.
        I could have stayed up all night telling you
and you and you and you
        what I don't mean to do,
and then carried off a shiny invisible
        ghost life through the performative dew,
and finished with a glance and a dismount,
        a behind the back dribble, or a last twirl.

So let am not be as it never meant
        to be, no warrant
for pretty or fit or memory or esteem.
        Let the wish break up with the fact,
sending letters on Sundays in little blue obsolescent
        envelopes, in tiny print.
Let a man and a boy and a girl whose torso is
        a testament to metamorphosis
tell their own tales but as for me
        I am not and I am not going to be.
Thank you for listening. Once or twice
        I did come close. I was almost a flirty girl.

GENO

A long safe life, or glory
and an early grave. Like our silver-gray runt of a cat
who can sulk in his tent, who will hide after every bath,
who stood in our kitchen in triumph, once, having mangled a wren;
who ran out the door again, tonight, and has not yet come home;
who wanted attention, like the wisecracking basketball coach—
Italian, not Greek, and quite mortal—from whom we took his name.

TEXT MESSAGES

See unused marble in its
Roman quarry, halted on its way uphill.

• • •

The flowers we grow for their scent
never smell as sweet
as those we find along the road,
but the latter die so fast, indoors.

• • •

Rosehips in top-heavy clusters at red lights
along our traffic median,
their tart flesh no doubt poisoned from its air.

• • •

Thanks to ten dollar per gallon gasoline,
I now have time to think while I wait for the bus.

• • •

We look at the sloth and ask: *How does she get so much done?*

• • •

Try again and again and invest very little each time—
one evolutionary strategy; but is it ever a plan for art?
Mosquitoes lay their eggs
in clusters over shrinking ponds—
a thousand memos in a typing pool.

• • •

The steeple, so solemn and so
caught up in its one task,
never does make it all the way past the cloud.

. . .

Schloss
She wanted to make
a 35mm film about Rilke,
about how pointless it must have seemed to him
to wait for inspiration in that castle
while the war—
but she never found the time.

. . .

To Notebooks
We found our ideas when they were made
of marble, and have left them all of brick.

. . .

Introns
Behold the humanities library's long shelves,
each hardback tagged like bands on DNA—
some of the code thus labeled spells out all life;
most of the rest of it never gets read at all.

SELF-PORTRAIT AS MUPPET

Beleaguered
administrators
everywhere, I am one of you.
I came from a swamp too.
It was hard to get out, even harder to be young and green
and try to please children, but hardest of all to learn

how to run the whole show: I nevertheless remain
supposedly in sole charge
of a dance marathon, a masochistic
acrobat, a pig addicted to lipstick
who holds black belts in several martial arts,
a talking shag rug eight feet tall, a bear
who tries and tries and fails to entertain,

a pantomime horse whose parts
refuse to leave their DayGlo yard,
a rock band, and a Pepto-Bismol colored pair
of cows from Mars who only know one song,
Mahna mahna, whatever that means.
                                        I need a rest.
I sigh, I sag, I shrug in my canvas chair
and perk up again to chat with tonight's special guest,
who asks me why my eyes bug out. Go figure.

I used to sit on a wall
all day and read the news. Now we go on
in ten, and I am happy to tell
you what almost anyone
who seems to be running things
will say once you catch us backstage: somebody bigger
than we can ever get is pulling the strings.

THE SOUL

Easy to recognize in its costume
made up of Sunday puzzles and Scrabble tiles,

you can take it, but not very far.
Nor can you baste, drip-dry or evaluate

happily what's left when it's removed.

Respectable people have found it in a guitar.
Consider where it lives, or hides, in you.

IN MEMORY OF THE ROCK BAND BREAKING CIRCUS

You were whiny and socially unacceptable even
to loud young men whose first criterion
for rock and roll was that it strike someone else
as awful and repulsive and you told
grim stories about such obscure affairs
as a man-killing Zamboni and a grudge-
laden marathon runner from Zanzibar

who knifed a man after finishing sixteenth

Each tale sped from you at such anxious rate
sarcastic showtunes abject similes
feel like a piece of burnt black toast
for example *threaded on a rusty wire* followed
up by spitting *too much time to think*
by fusillades from rivetguns by cold
and awkward bronze reverberant church bells

percussive monotones 4/4 all for

the five or six consumers who enjoyed
both the impatience of youth
and the pissiness of middle age
as if you knew you had to get across
your warnings against all our lives as fast
as practicable before roommate or friend
could get up from a couch to turn them off

We barely remember you in Minnesota we love

our affable Replacements who modeled a more
acceptable form of rage who thought of girls
and cities boys and beds and homes and cars

as flawed but fixable with the right drink
right mates and right guitar strings whereas you
did not and nothing in your songs resolved
except in a certain technical sense as a drill

resolves contests between drywall and screw

Your second bassist took the stage name Flour
your second drummer copied a machine
Somebody else in your hometown took credit
for every sound you taught them how to use
I write about you now since nobody else
is likely to and since even appalled
too-serious flat compliments like these

are better than nothing and because to annoy

perseverate and get under everyone's skin
beats the hell out of the real worst thing in the world
which is to fade into silence entirely which
will never happen to *The Ice Machine*
to "Driving the Dynamite Truck" to *The Very Long Fuse*
to *Smoker's Paradise* such hard sticks thrown
in the eyes of any audience that is

I should say not until it happens to me

3

También las piedras son el rio.

—Octavio Paz, "Mudra"

DULLES ACCESS ROAD

Seen from the paid-for
taxicab on the way
to the paid-for flight,

this is our preparation for
the world, which insists
on employment, which insists,

if you want adults
to take you seriously,
that you have to make somebody

pay. We are untrained
to manage even the pace
at which we live. Slow down at the last red light,

its monochrome certainty ordinary
for it, but never for us,
though it swings on wires nearly within human reach;

behind it, as they do
almost every day at this hour,
impregnable metal containers dissolve in the sky.

TARMAC WITH SOUNDTRACK

Passive and well-guarded,
The china-white airplanes await the signal to roll,
Each on its own
Low surface, hundreds of yards
Between them, with no people in their flat view,
Only the grinding of refueling carts
And opaque glints from portholes and from wings.

We like to follow instructions, unless we dislike
The people who are giving them. "We'd like
To celebrate a frequent customer
Who has experienced a momentous occasion:
Happy fiftieth birthday, Dolores Soap!"
Unanimous, restless passengers applaud.

While this world is, in fact, so marvelous
That only works of art approach the praise
Its flavorful, tart intricacies demand,
The truths of our lives in it are so grim
That we can tolerate them only if
They come to us in the relatively
Impenetrable fuselages of art.
Preparations continue for cloud cover. Baby names lift

Their possibilities in the short air, in which
We hear spare songs with no
Spare parts: less than harmonious, even detuned,
They play the drums with mallets, and guitars
With forks and spoons, the kind
Of approximate music you once believed you would make,
Before you thought you might make none at all.

OVER CONNECTICUT

Inland, the antique milemarkers spread
themselves out into twentieth-century lanes,

jammed up this afternoon, though built for speed—
sun-harmed, old news, old toys, they bury the lede

of Prudence Crandall's schoolroom heritage,
her kettle of cider, her wishes traced by hand.

We miss her now. We parcel out her land.
Town halls fade into greenery like spies.

New London's keeping Groton in its sights;
its drawbridge swings, a military career.

New Haven is old scores and old concrete,
old freeways where the Great Migration stalled;

the Sound turns agate, band by frozen band.
By Haddam, there are only Linens 'n Things

and other things, great mounds, whole civilizations
still glowing in faint spits along Route Nine . . .

I miss the Great Society with its sense
that we could redraw maps that ailed us, gone

in a mist of real estate and demonstrations,
three or four angry years before I was born.

AN ATLAS OF THE ATLAS MOTH

Now I am an adult & I will never eat again.
All the weight & elaboration that ever took in
a morsel of anything
save air & sex have fallen away
& remain in my soft cocoon, whose lost array

of silk will last longer than I do. In Taiwan, a girl
can take it to market, pin ribbons on it, & fill
it with a few brass coins.
As for me, saturnine, spread out & almost
immobile as long as the sun shines, I am host

to a fleet of sparkles: slightly awry, divided
in half by my own body, I can bide
my time on any leaf
or parked car's hood, till lights outdoors grow
cool & breeze sends me down again into my slow

glide in search of a mate. There are parts of me
that anyone can see through. Transparency
like mica occupies
my awkward fourfold wings. I am nearly hollow:
wind, love & oblivion veer up & down, & I follow.

SWINGLINE STAPLER

Likeness held in the hand,
I can link any thin thing
to any thin thing: rarely cold
to touch, and unassuming not withstand-
ing my silver paint's sparkle, I can connect
a map of Connect-
icut to an atlas of Iceland,
or flatten out the mountains of Vermont.
I have no use for a doctrine of non-
attachment, although I once
put an argument for it together:
I see through and remember any sliver
of paper or ribbon that has ever passed
between my stainless teeth . . .

In hope that what I join
nobody will put asunder,
I preside eagerly over
every union I encounter; I pretend
that anything I make fast,
will hold fast, though the ever-
sharper incisors of my mother,
Time, her servant, Dust, and her other
servants, Water and Sunlight—
the enemies of the news
today, and of anything you write
tomorrow—will in fact devour
everything I touch:
each letter and artifact
will go the way of all files—
cursive and print will join up,

gold and black merge with indigo,
each stock and weight at last
as good as any other in
the empty chamber I will someday know.

PROTHALAMION WITH LAOCOÖN SIMULACRUM

for Amanda Schaffer, science writer, and Dennis Potami, sculptor

Everything good is a challenge: your plastic casts
that tax the calmest model, the sensitive electronic wrists
of the robots that lift the casts, the lithe
and programmed curves by which your software makes
apparent to our analog gaze the myth
of a prophet who told the truth and wrestled snakes.

Today is your handiwork too, and everything flaunts
its goodness for you: you have become your own
informative heralds, supernatural pair
empowered to move us by dozens, friends and aunts
transported where needed through country lanes and midair,
so that it is not even a breach of tone

to speak of you and wish you well past dark.
A marriage, like a body, can be made
in a cocoon or a frenzy, but yours
is not: it is a part-instinctive braid
of space and work that feels nothing like work,
elusive and durable like the dinosaur's

bone in *Bringing Up Baby,* whose principals wrestle
each other, timetables and claims for romantic love—
what it may do and how it might evolve,
how it can climb a pediment or pestle
through microfine adhesions, how to live
as something more than psychological fossils,

advancing always the more persuasive news
that we create each other, works in progress.
So ligaments evolved for us to use
flirtatiously, as a lover might stretch a toe

to touch a lover under a notional table,
a secular altar made of skirts and glass:

there's more of you in love than we can know.
Say love is like a ligament, is able
to bind with more than chemical attraction,
to bend and turn, to take most sorts of stress—
so hard to model, shaped by such selection
to hold you together and take you where you want to go.

LIVING NEXT TO THE RIVER

José Luis Rivas: "Un río"

From the height of their rock
the little boys throw seeds.
Out from the mud, quicksilver bits run
all the way to the shade of a barrel afloat:
only its dim plastic skin
can fancy itself cool
in this scorching noon that fills
the space where a breeze should be
and burns or blinds the silent ripples' sides.
No motorboat cuts through,
extending its wake like a river all its own . . .

The littlest children entertain themselves
by trapping crayfish under rocks;
they kneel on the slimy flats to inspect their catch.

You walk upstream,
head under the old wooden bridge (of course it creaks),
and remember last year's floods,
when even the brewery warehouse—stuck so high up there—
still knuckled under to the rising mud.
Other buildings on the shore now hold
the waters' brilliant-yellow patina.
And your heart, too, swells at times
with a kind of pride in it,
like a ship in full sail, or a frigate-bird in heat . . .

It's your town, after all. It belongs to the river;
you do, too. A droplet of sweat
zips down your forehead, then dissipates
before it can fall to the water.
                                        Above the rail,

you know you could easily cry
instead, and you turn away—
like someone who puts out a lamp,
then leans on the windowsill
to see the lit-up stars all night through rain.

SUNDAY AFTERNOON IN CHAPULTEPEC PARK

Alberto Blanco: "Un domingo por la tarde en Chapultepec"

Already the afternoon falls and the multitude
loses itself in the tunnel to the Metro
clouds threaten us and themselves

The flagpole looks deserted
the monument to the boy-soldier heroes too
the pushcarts with their candy and ices still sound
and the little ones crying and laughing

Foul smells come from the cages at the zoo
and a hostile posse making a racket
shouting their discontent at the top of their lungs
their will to live their will to die

A pinwheel vendor with black glasses
a chubby woman minding a chubby boy
the sun comes and goes
comes and goes
the soldiers pass among the citizens
conspicuous in khaki

Kids pass on rollerskates sliding as if they moved
along the stone edge of a riverbed
they meet and they speed away
zigzag and see themselves twist
through the hall of mirrors
the sun takes it hard

Cotton candy in chemical roses
skates with pollen-yellow clouds for wings
boats brimful with trash
(the crowd has moved away)

trees dry despite recent rain
shawls newly washed
plastic sandals juiceboxes Coke cans
yo-yos Pepsis Frisbees stale hot dogs

Along the pavement the rest
of the improvisatory banquet
cigar wrappers
unfortunate Lotto slips
fruits with one bite taken out or chewed down to a core
gum and cardboard boxes
among lubricious whistles oaths and lies
shouts of pain shouts of release
timid confessions of love

Ghost Rider in flames on the shirt of a metalhead boy
a rainbow on his girlfriend's little breasts
it follows the afternoon while the afternoon lasts
past the shops selling boiled sweets
the cops' beat-up jeep
guitar music same as always
the tennis shoes in every conceivable color
the same thirst the same resentment we keep coming back
here the trick is not to collapse
the trick is to lose oneself
a vanishing
into the vanished crowd

THERE

Like waking from something, but not from a dream

      so sleepy
there was really nothing there.
I had to pull over right away,
get off the road.

In Lebanon, New Hampshire,
which is not an example,
a bridge with an upward curve like a lowercase n,
rises above the terrestrial
road surface, beautiful guardrails, beautiful sun

      hills
like rehearsal curtains,
thick and heavy, a uniform green.
There's a ten-speed bike on a gingerbread porch,
its handbrakes askew like the talons of bats,

            an Infant of Prague House.
The wooden sign says only *Rooms*.

The sky is a word. The sky is a womb. The sky
befits a summer afternoon
with somewhere else I ought to be,
but not yet.

Two girls in oversized running shoes find
each other and, looking sullen together,
disappear over the rise,

while pale strips of cloud soothe the *Nouveauté
Boutique,* Hisick's Clothing and Uniforms

(on show: a firefighter's uniform)
and the Back to School Sale conducted
from a tent in rescue orange,

across the street from the LISTEN thrift store.
The rest of the clouds just go, passing lightly, carefully
over the town and my life as well, telling
it gently, *There now,* or just *There.*

KENDALL SQUARE IN THE RAIN

What we can't say openly
we say in poetry,

speaking about another as myself.

Who has the right
to say who has the right?

Where else but in the negative
space of the empty de facto amphitheater,
the shade of the pre-stressed concrete or the shadow
of the Hatch Shell, shall I go
to register a complaint?

Speak to the flat grass, Midas,
about your ass's ears,
about your wish to embarrass
your friends with a ribbon and bow.

Speak out against self-pity
during the playground games,
bouncing a loud rubber ball. See how that goes.

You could have been the king, and now you are.

There is a promise in compromise,
and two I's in disguise,
and a series of curtains the downpour pulls up
over the flat black grates
that keep the water from clambering into the building,
the building where you might work; they protect it from floods,
precipitation hammering childish channels
into the packed-down flotsam, the wadded-up
mud like forgetfulness, driving the new twigs home.

STORROW DRIVE IN THE SUN

Citgo sign, we love you,
though we do feel guilty about it;
we used to believe the city paid your bills.
All that neon, and the color off too,
            not red; red-orange.

Big—I mean big: three stories!—or say expansive,
though they also look expensive, windows
too sadly square to look residential,
too glassy, too showy, to fit a factory.
Maybe they make the sun shine on all the ideas.
They hatch ideas from eggs,
round, pockmarked, translucent eggs,
each one the height of a four-year-old child.

Really, though, children are taller than ideas.
And nobody *has* ideas
the way you can *have* a baby: they just come to you
like rock doves who pace on a roof,
then settle, then fly away
becoming pigeons in ten thousand years,
then iridescing to beat the band.
                        O self-important hub,
you fit me more than any other where.
Both of us seem to require minor repair.
O brass boathouse angel, O white on green arrows, looking
down on me from inner suburbs' signs . . .

Keep more water safe, river,
away from the rowers. It's OK if you want to freeze.

OCEAN STATE JOB LOT

No one is going to make
    much more of this stuff now, or ever again.

Graceless in defeat
    but beautiful, harmless and sad
on shelves that overlap like continents,

these Cookie Monster magnets, miniature
    monster trucks, scuffed multiple Elmos, banners

that say NO FEAR
    and A GRILL FOR EVERY BOY
are a feast for every sense.

Some would be bad manners
    to give or to bring home—

so many pounds of oysters, so many gallons of franks and beans . . .
    It is a sea
that we discover out here,

where every piece of evidence
    has a notional price and a buyer, and we find our own
among its premises:

a hundred cans of pepper relish shaped
    like lobster pots,
a big glass pickle meant to keep coins in,

a gleaming square whose effervescent
    label promises
the taste of the Atlantic in a tin.

OVER WINGAERSHEEK BEACH

Nathan's kite shows a pattern of angelfish, coral, and sea stars
                                        on its shimmery underside,

so that the higher up it goes,
                    the more the twine plays out, stays taut, ascends,

the farther down we seem to be,
                                        between the glossy focus

and the substance of the sea, and the sea floor,
                    so that, as I bring the kite down in the heat of the day,

turning the strung loop over on its spool,
                    it looks as if we were rising toward a surface that came slowly

down to meet us, a sky refashioned as water so clear
                                        that we could almost take it in,

could almost move spontaneously, by
                    accident, up to that easy, cool, breathable air.

HELPLESSNESS

August 2008

The dozens of Canada geese in search
Of foliage over the school field stand at ease
And yet in militant formation,
Ready to replace
Us here and for all our territory

At dusk, when all the soccer players leave.
Nathan thinks the goalposts
Are all letters: big white H, great yellow Y,
And so they are.
There is no constellation called the Goose

Nor the Swarm of Geese,
Ready to follow one star over all the dead sky.
Today with every threat of summer
Rain I can imagine half New England
Underwater, Washington, DC's

Sad August fog 500 miles north
Or Greenland's ice in slivers out at sea.
And I can't stop myself, this summer, looking
Five times daily at graphs
That pretend to predict the nation: their digital tide

Keeps rising and falling over the rickety locks.
Today it's a tie, 44
To 44. The pixellated, duelling
Numerals stick out their necks
Like hungry standing birds.

The geese alight
At ease, a scatterplot.

So noble their work together, far over our heads . . .
They will leave for good soon, replaced
Only by other geese
Who breathe our air, immune to our concern.

BRUSSELS SPROUTS ON THE STALK

Leaf-fringe for sills and stairs
and veins for tiny windows, they become
arcologies: apartment-clusters found
in science fiction from the seventies,
when everyone lived in towers a mile high,
rode vertically to work or school by tram,
and could not touch the ground
for fear of all the toxic outdoor air.

Green variables, they lose
their rougher outer leaf
when handled or subjected to the heat
of oven, saucepan or a bright July.
Our old plans fail; our new ones are too slight
to register. Above our stove, we try
to recognize our grief
or call to mind our fear
about our own green globe,
whose temperature rises year by year.

THE FUTURE

A baby bottle packed with Scrabble tiles.

The hood of a Chevy turned into a planter for maize,
askew in an alley. The varicolored stalks
compete in the shade for attention from the one sun.

Alectryomancy in the bulk food aisle.

Double vision: the street as it is—
foot traffic and wind, and bargains at Black Ink—
and as it might be under a foot of rain,
fine algae lapping the base for the merchants' tables,
impassable stoops, bales of waterlogged books,

a convention of periwigged ghosts.

The Jurassic air. The Atlantic coast.

Grease and ozone, the faint scents that reassure engineers.

The triumph hidden in each wheelchair ramp:
such heavy inconvenience overcome
after so many patient years.

The longest escalator in New England,
its endless rows of teeth at Porter Square
set just above the water table,
so far and no farther into the ground.

CHLOROPHYLL

Rain at varying rates
Breaks up the queues at our bus stop; most people who know
They waited too long to buy umbrellas can stand,
But some sit down on rocks,
While overhead, on long
Clouds sharpened like blades on skates,
We see pneumonia weather sliding in.

All nature seems to be at work
Reluctantly, as this Friday's anxious
Managers, both desultory and eager
To clear their stacked-up paper out of the way,
Go home. Do not start anything today.
Pay less attention to politics. Wrap it all up.
Consider the neighbor whose overstuffed

Three-story house caught fire from inside,
Who saved cards, check stubs, apple wrappers, news,
Who would have gone up
In a fireball had the fire trucks arrived
Five minutes late: we saw him just
This morning, smiling
At us in his loose sweater, out on the curb

Beside one of his indoor-outdoor cats.
Behind them, all unharmed, we saw his row
Of lilies, opalescent, deaf to us
And focused on their arduous life cycle
Of evapotranspiration:
They work all day, each day, with outstretched
Ignorant leaves that might as well be hands.

HYPERBOREA

after Pindar

Once past the man-high teeth
and the disintegrating ice
that separate human lands
from the gods' secret territory, what Herakles found
was nothing on first sight worth even half a breath
to the sort of fortune-tellers and singers who vaunt
celebrities' pleasures, who promise new heroes the solace
of willing nymphets and smooth-shouldered boys,
then give them marble busts and sapphire crowns.
Behind the curtain of snows
lay temperate air and a firepit, and
what heroes, after labors, really want:
a couple of apple trees; a brook; warm shade where hardwoods stand;
a stump for a table; crisp weather; a place to sit down.

EL NIDO

Some say that the thing most beautiful
in this world is a fleet of trim sailing ships,
the kind we saw on the horizon,
or a phalanx in close formation, whose flashing spears
make the sun brighter as it sets,
                                    but I
now say the most beautiful thing is the whole of the view
from the stucco roof of a hotel
in Puerto Vallarta, Jalisco, Mexico,
the roof we found twice up a century
of stairs, past bright blue tempera and tiles,
the hotel Los Cuatro Vientos, the Four Winds,
the roof where those winds finesse
one another and cross in the tropics' hospitable air,
the air that knows nothing of winter, the winds that meet
across the rooftop bar called El Nido, the Nest,
with its pair of unprepossessing steel tables and chairs,
its avocados in a low steel dish:
the most beautiful thing that exists or has ever existed
on the face of the globe, the globe the winds enfold—
not for the green and irregular curve of the Sierra Madre, or Mother of
                                    Mountains, foothills
to the east, however crossed with streaks of bronze;
not because the sun cut the cathedral's metal hat,
its cheerful crown of wires, antennas, and arcs
so silver at noon, then almost fluorescent at dusk;
not because the same
sun swept like a flat stone
across the stepwise hills' clay lemniscates
of tiles and wasps'-nests walls, each lighting up
the next, so that they burned, and were not consumed;
not because the neon commerce
farther down did nothing to harm

the Bahia de Banderas, or Bay of Flags;
not because the Malecón, or promenade
at the side of the beach, arranged the scene in thirds,
dividing the near-unbroken violet sea from the town's unruly white
and tan,
as sunset stitched that same sea to the air;
but only because, in that view,
you were:
the gold of some summer
returned to your hair in December,
the perfect fit your off-white linen shirt,
a few brisk clouds in back of you
like ricepaper cut-outs of doves,
and me without our camera,
having promised to bring it, then left it a mile away,
so that the only way
to copy out even a scrim
of the scene for other eyes than yours and mine
is just to put some small part of it into writing
for you: here, then, are these lines.

BIFROST

Not mine, but somebody's Heaven: half a moon,
        laughter through the quad, and cloudlessness
without a verb; a shouted recipe;

        this visible world a pause,
a rise of one degree.
        A tan cat settles comfortably

on cement; ungrateful diamond-angled
        sun casts its patterns of vacuums against a flat roof.
How finely weighted in my favor

        most of our contests in this life have been.
The last red trees are opals, are from Mars,
        whose light takes twenty minutes to arrive

& then gets lost. Leaves fly and crowd above
        the soccer players' shins, rich brittle grass
as high as it will be

        this year, & free
on every path, slow, unassuming
        shadows dig in, to shut the long gate of the day.

FLOODED MEADOW

Low dandelion leaves are zoned commercial,
with their promise of puffballs to come.

Bits of dew spackle the high grass
asymmetrically; they are sleek apartment windows,
    skyscrapers are weeds.

Tall sprigs of goldenrod patrol
the blown-down city line. . . .

There is another world
in this world, but it was not made for you.

Round oniongrass stalks are old monuments
to persistence in hard times.
    You could live up inside one
and learn to like it, cramped quarters,
    cooking smells and all.

Two bees report on traffic, warning listeners
to the anemophily channel
    as the natural disaster
of humanity comes closer
    every morning. Work while you can, they say.

BUTTERFLY WITH PARACHUTE

A real one wouldn't need one,
but the one Nathan draws surely does:
four oblongs the size and color of popsicles,
green apple, toasted coconut and grape,
flanked, two per side, by billowing valentine hearts,
in a frame of Scotch tape.
Alive, it could stay off the floor,
for a few unaerodynamic minutes;
thrown as a paper airplane, for one or two more.

Very sensibly, therefore,
our son gave it something, not to keep it apart
from the ground forever, but rather to make safe its descent.
When we ask that imagination discover the limits
of the real
world only slowly,
maybe this is what we meant.

NOTES AND THANKS

Thanks to all at Graywolf Press, and also at Harvard University Press, Rain Taxi Editions, Harry Tankoos Press, and Columbia University Press, for their help with previous books; thanks to Macalester College and to Harvard University for their support more generally during the years in which these poems came about.

Thanks to the writers and editors through whose commissions some poems began, among them Forrest Gander, who asked me to adapt Mexican poems, including those by Alberto Blanco and José Luis Rivas (Mariana Saavedra improved my Spanish); to Jonathan Farmer of *At Length*, through whose Telephone Project "Owl Music" began; to Amanda and Dennis, who asked for an epithalamium; to Tim Trace Peterson, co-editor of *Troubling the Line*; to Caleb Klaces of *Like Starlings*.

My boundless thanks to Jessica Bennett, who provided the title for "Reverse Deciduous Existence" and the affection and intellect for so much else, and to Nathan, and to Cooper.

My thanks also to more friends and allies who gave helpful advice and encouragement with some of the poems: David Blair, Dan Bouchard, Jeffrey and Sandra Burt, Dan Chiasson, Heather Dubrow, Jordan Ellenberg, Kelly Everding, Sarah Fox, Jorie Graham, Nick Halpern, H. L. Hix, Erin Kottke, Jennifer Lewin, Eric Lorberer, Sara Marcus, Mary Matze, Thomas McNeely, Ange Mlinko, Alissa Quart, Donald Revell, John Redmond, Michael Scharf, Jeff Shotts, Craig Teicher, Rachel Trousdale, and Monica Youn.

"To Subarus": see Harvey Karp, *The Happiest Baby on the Block* (2003).

"When the Sweet Wind Did Gently Kiss the Trees": see *The Merchant of Venice*, V.i.2.

"Draft Camp": basketball players likely but not certain to be selected in a pro draft congregate for pickup games and other demonstrations of talent before team scouts. Draft camp (also called pre-draft camp) takes place in the WNBA and in the NBA. WNBA fans may spot players who were or would have been in the 2005 and 2006 drafts, among them Janel McCarville, Kendra Wecker, Cathrine Kraayeveld, the late Shawntinice Polke, Katy Feenstra, Sherill Baker, Kristin Haynie, Barbara Turner, and Laurie Koehn.

"Two Victorian Scenes": the Victorian photographer Lady Hawarden has won renewed attention not least for the many portraits she made of her daughters; see Virginia Dodier, *Lady Hawarden: Studies from Life* (London: Victoria and Albert Museum, 1998) or Carol Mayor, *Becoming* (Durham, N.C.: Duke Univ. Press, 1999).

"Self-Portrait as Muppet": in addition to Kermit the Frog, the poem refers to *The Muppet Movie*, to Gonzo, Miss Piggy, Sweetums, Fozzy Bear, and the Electric Mayhem, and to several running gags from both *Sesame Street* and *The Muppet Show*.

"In Memory of the Rock Band Breaking Circus": the song about the runner, "Knife in the Marathon," may be found on *The Very Long Fuse*, Breaking Circus's first album, which used a drum machine. Founded by Steve Bjorklund in Chicago in the early 1980s, Breaking Circus moved to Minneapolis and recorded two more albums there, with Todd Trainer on drums and Flour on bass.

"An Atlas of the Atlas Moth" owes details to an exhibit at the Boston Museum of Science, 2008. Native to Southeast Asia, the Atlas moth is the largest known moth.

"Storrow Drive in the Sun": contrary to widespread belief, the city of Boston does not, in fact, pay to light the CITGO sign.

"Brussels Sprouts on the Stalk": "science fiction from the seventies": for example, Robert Silverberg, *The World Inside* (1971).

"Hyperborea" adapts some lines from Pindar's Third Olympian Ode.

"El Nido": the first few lines echo the first few lines of Sappho's fragment 16.

STEPHEN BURT is the author of two previous books of poetry, *Parallel Play* and *Popular Music,* which won the Colorado Prize. He is also the author of several works of critical nonfiction, including *Close Calls with Nonsense: Reading New Poetry,* which was a finalist for the National Book Critics Circle Award in criticism. His essays and reviews have appeared in the *Believer,* the *London Review of Books,* the *Nation,* the *New York Times Book Review,* and the *Times Literary Supplement,* among other newspapers and journals. He is Professor of English at Harvard University, and he lives in Belmont, Massachusetts.

The text of the poems in *Belmont* have been set in Méridien, a typeface designed in 1954 by Adrian Frutiger. Book design by Kim R. Doughty. Composition by BookMobile Design & Digital Publisher Services, Minneapolis, Minnesota. Manufactured by Versa Press on acid-free 30 percent postconsumer wastepaper.